"Fight The Good Fight of Faith"

"Fight The Good Fight of Faith"

Dr. R. Michael Baldock

Library of Congress Control Number: 2021922795

PAPERBACK: 978-1-956803-57-0
EBOOK: 978-1-956803-58-7

All scripture used is from the King James Version of the Bible unless otherwise noted. All Hebrew and Greek definitions were from the New Strong's Expanded, Exhaustive Concordance of the Bible.

Ordering Information:

For orders and inquiries, please contact:
1-888-404-1388
www.goldtouchpress.com
book.orders@goldtouchpress.com

Printed in the United States of America

CONTENTS

INTRODUCTION

I am sure that every believer is aware that they are in warfare. In order to **"fight the good fight of faith"** one must be aware of who and what the enemy is. Too often we battle one another which is not really the battle that should we should be fighting. The real battle is coming from spiritual forces with the intent of removing the believer from their faith walk.

We are in a spiritual warfare and it is intense. The church is being attacked from every angle. Believers are engaged in this spiritual warfare and many are weak because of it. Satan thrives upon the weaknesses of the believers. At the time of writing this book the world has been facing a pandemic for well over a year. When this pandemic broke out fear began running rampant I saw fear hit the Christian (Church World) like nothing I had ever seen before. We have always had to fight against fear, but this was somewhat different. This fight has seemingly taken its toll on the masses. Many Churches have closed their doors to never open them again. **My greatest concern is, many are losing the tenacity to fight the good fight of faith!**

In this book we are going to reveal (although not exhaustive) some of the areas the enemy works. Along with just how to combat (fight) what the enemy throws at the believer.

In my opinion, one of the greatest areas the enemy works within, is the ignorance of the believer. Ignorance is a killer however that killer can be removed through the illumination and revelation of the Word of God. Knowledge of the Word along with the application is something that Satan and his minions try to keep the believer from receiving.

Another area that I believe that the enemy uses that I have noticed is the lack of knowing how to live for God. There is also a lack of experiencing (living daily in) the **Victory of the Cross and the Finished Work of Jesus Christ.**

Within this small book I hope to bring revelation (a ***Rhema*** Word) to make the Word come alive and active within every reader, along with some keys to a **'life of Victory!'**

CHAPTER 1

The Enemies of Faith Part 1 (Satan and his minions)

"For we wrestle no against flesh and blood, but against principalities against powers, against the rulers of darkness of this world, against spiritual wickedness in high places" Ephesians 6:12

Before we begin to dig a little deeper concerning spiritual warfare I want to first establish that every enemy and every demonic force was defeated at the Cross and through the Finished Work of Jesus Christ. In reality, we are facing a foe that has been stripped of its (his) authority.

"And having spoiled principalities and powers (stripping Satan all of his minions of any authority because of the Atoning work of Jesus Christ at Calvary) He made a show of them openly(the victory that Jesus Christ brought was not done in secret nor within a shadow but was done openly on the Cross of Calvary) triumphing over them in

> *it (the victory that Christ brought to the believing
> sinner was one of ultimate victory which brings
> the believer into a life of "Abundant living" John
> 10:10; Romans 6:4 which is the Newness of life)
> Colossians 2:15 Emphasis Mine*

The only real authority that Satan and his demonic forces have is the authority that the believer relinquishes. I am certainly not trying to minimize demonic forces. However, it is important for every believer to come to the realization that their victory is in the Cross and stop giving the enemy room to work.

> **"Neither give place (any position of opportunity)
> to the Devil.) Ephesians 4:27**

Let's examine the different levels of influences that Satan uses against the believer.

1. **Against Principalities;** This term is from the Greek word ***"Archas"*** which refers to the highest ranking of Satan's kingdom. They are also known as the angels that followed the uprising of Satan (Daniel 10:13, 20).

2. **Against Powers;** From the Greek word ***"Exousia"*** meaning permissible power; permission, authority, right, liberty, power to do anything. These particular powers get their authority from the high ranking principalities within Satan's kingdom. Their powers and authority become intensified as the believer opens doors from them to operate.

3. **Against the rulers of the darkness of this world.** The word **"rulers"** is from the Greek word, "Kosmokratopas"

meaning those who carry out the ruling of the Powers i.e. the spirit world rulers. These are those who are under the power of the *"principalities and powers"* **who are ruled by Satan and his minions.**

4. **Against spiritual (wicked spirits) wickedness in high (heavenly) places.** These wicked spirits are demon spirits that war against the believer. These demon spirits use a multitude of weapons within their arsenal some of which are: depression, oppression (a born again spirit filled child of God cannot be demon possessed) low self-esteem, fear and anxiety to mention just a few. The great news is, through the Cross and the Finished Work of Jesus Christ the believer has VICTORY!

The following are some other things that these spirits will try to use against the believer through their evil influences. Take careful notice, the very tool the enemy will use in each of the following is ignorance concerning an understanding of the Word of God along with the Cross and the Finished Work of Jesus Christ! Ignorance is a killer! However, it can be removed through knowledge!

We are engaged in a tremendous spiritual battle and the time of passivity has passed, it is time to go to battle against all of the methods of the enemy. One of the ways to engage Satan and his minions is, to become familiar with his character and mindset. It is important to understand the mind of your enemy. With that in mind, let's take a moment to gain some important insight to Satan.

The great prophet Ezekiel gives some great insight to Satan in the 28th chapter of his writings. Although this chapter deals with judgment that was coming to the Prince of Tyrus, it reveals a clear picture of Lucifer and his mindset.

"The Word of the Lord came again unto me, saying (regarding the spirit world, this Chapter is one of the most remarkable in the Bible. As the Holy Spirit through Ezekiel had concerned Himself with the city, He now concerns Himself with its ruler, who is symbolic of Satan. In fact, this Chapter, in combination with Isa., Chapt.14, gives s great insight into the ruler of darkness, Lucifer), The Expositor's Study Bible Jimmy Swaggart

Beginning in verse 2 the heart of the wicked one is revealed; His heart is lifted (exalted) while he tries to set his heart as the Heart of God. Even though this is speaking directly concerning the heart of the 'Prince of Tyrus,' there is little doubt that it is Satan who energizing him as a victim of his cruelty. This can be said, because the character of the Prince is driven by **'Pride'** which is the very foundation of sin which is without a doubt the character of Satan.

Verse 3 speaks of him being wiser than Daniel with no secret kept from him. In reality, he only thinks that his wisdom surpasses Daniel, he was only wise in his own eyes. It was within his own thinking that no secret was hid from him. While he may know the Word of God he is certainly not privy to all of its revelations.

Verse 4 thru 5 speaks of his wisdom and knowledge bringing him great riches. In comparison, Daniel was concerned about carrying out the will of God, while those under the influence of Satan are after earthly gain which causes them to be lifted up within their own hearts.

Verse 6 reveals Satan's desire to be God and that desire becomes within those that follow him, and that includes man in this present day. Verses 7-10 reveal the downfall (how Satan will (was) be brought down) of Lucifer (Satan).

As we continue in this great chapter, it gives more detailed description of Satan; Notice the phrase in verse 12; *"you seal up the sum of wisdom"* this phrase reveals Lucifer as the wisest most beautiful **'Angel'** created by God, and served God in Holiness and righteousness for a period of time.

The phrase; *"Perfect in beauty"* again, this portrays Lucifer as the most beautiful Angelic being created. The Holy Spirit even labeled his beauty as, *'perfect.'* Even though the King of Tyrus is used in a symbolic form, these particular statements, in no way refer to a mere mortal man. It obviously is referring to Lucifer (Satan).

The phrase in verse 13; *"He was in the Garden of Eden"* is an interesting statement. This is not referring to the Garden of Eden where God placed Adam. In fact, it is referring to a Garden that was in the world before the creation of Adam.

The phrase also in verse 13; *"Every precious stone was his covering;"* This statement is very close to the garments that the Priests of Israel wore.

The phrase in verse 13; *He was the leader of worship and was referred to as "O Lucifer, son of the morning."* Of course, this was how Lucifer fell (Job 38:4; Isa. 14:12)

The phrase; *"Anointed Cherub who covered"* most likely refers once again to Lucifer as the leader of *'Worship.'*

The phrase in verse 15; *"He was perfect in all his ways until 'iniquity' was found in him."* Lucifer created that iniquity within himself, which was the result of being exalted by his own **'pride!'**

<u>Satan's Rebellion</u>

The great Prophet Isaiah records Satan's rebellion (war) against God. In Isaiah Chapter 14:12 there are three questions brought to Lucifer (Satan).

1. **"How did you fall from Heaven," "O Lucifer (Satan) son of the morning?"**

2. **"How are you cast down to the ground?"**

3. **"What did weaken you?"**

The answer to these questions, are revealed in verse 13; His fall was the results of his **'Five I Wills.'**

1. **"I will ascend into Heaven!"**

2. **"I will exalt my throne above the stars of God!"**

3. **"I will sit also upon the mount of the congregation in the sides of the North!"**

4. "I will ascend above the heights of the clouds!"

5. "I will be like the Most High!"

This rebellion no doubt took place before the creation of Adam. I believe that this created a catastrophic Judgment that is revealed between Genesis Chapter 1 verses 1and 2 leaving the world without form and void. There is little doubt (in my opinion) That there is a great possibility this was the time when demon spirits came into existence. They are possibly the disembodied spirits of the Pre-Adam creation. Some may say, "this is just a theory," well, give it some thought and study.

In Isaiah Chapter 14 verse 15 Satan is cast down to hell, to the depths of the Pit, with his final destination being the **'Lake of Fire!' (Rev.20:11-15).**

Satan now turns his fight against God's most prized creation, **'MAN!'** Genesis Chapter 3:1-5 reveals the beginning of this battle while using a serpent.

1. *"And he said unto the woman (Eve)"* it is evident that the serpent had the ability to speak, for, Eve was not taken back by the serpent speaking to her.

2. *"Yes, has God said, you shall eat of <u>every tree</u> of the garden?"* Notice, Satan purposely misquotes God, which he does continuously. This is the beginning of *'deceitfulness'* which is one of the greatest weapons of Satan. This was Eve's first mistake, she should had never engaged in a conversation with the serpent.

3. ***"And the woman (Eve) said unto the serpent"*** This was Eve's first mistake, she engaged in conversation with the serpent. Eve's second mistake was not **'RESISTING THE TEMPTER! (James 4:7-8)**

4. Eve continues her conversation with the serpent. ***"We may eat the fruit of the Garden, God said, You shall not eat of it, <u>neither shall you touch it</u>, lest you die."*** Eve's third mistake was adding to what God had originally spoken, which is, a big NO NO! Rev. 22:18-19

5. ***"And the serpent said unto the woman, You shall surely not die"*** In continuing with the conversation Satan continues to deceive Eve. His statement to her was a total denial of what God had originally spoken. He took the Word of God and twisted it into his own version, which was a total lie, many today are doing exactly the same thing. Remember, Satan is a liar and He never speaks the truth.

6. ***"For God does know that in the day you eat thereof then your eyes will be open."*** Satan is suggesting to Eve that man can reach a place of greater wisdom. Notice the attempt of Satan to speak directly to the pride of man. Man's pride is always searching for higher heights and deeper depths of this world which is an area that Satan uses today, that being stroking the pride of man.

7. ***"And you shall be gods, knowing good and evil"*** Satan is suggesting to Eve that man can become deity and know all things (becoming Omniscient). It seems the pattern of Satan is always directed to the pleasing of the Lust of the Eye, the Lust of the Flesh, the Pride of Life!

<u>Satan Tempts Jesus!</u>

"Then was Jesus led up of the Spirit into the wilderness to be tempted of the Devil." Matt. 4:1

Just after the Holy Spirit descending on Jesus, He was led by the Holy Spirit into a wilderness place to be tempted. This was an important part of the life of Jesus, He being, the last Adam (second man) was to be tempted in all areas like man is tempted (1 Cor. 15:21-22, 45, 47; Heb. 4:15). Let's examine each temptation and how Jesus reacted to it;

1. *"If you are the Son of God (the correct translation is; since you are the Son of God) command these stones to be bread"* Satan was tempting Jesus to use His own power and authority for His own benefit (no doubt he was hungry) which He was never to do nor did He ever do. When you look at strategy of Satan to get man to satisfy himself it seems to be working world wide. Man as always made it about himself, satisfying his own hunger and thirst. It is about ME, ME, ME!

   Jesus responded to this temptation saying, *"It is written, Man shall not live by bread alone, but by every Word that proceeds out of the Mouth of God!"* Jesus quoted, from Deut. 8:3 which reveals, the importance of man being dependent on God and every Word that He has spoken. The believer today must come to a knowledge of the Word of God most importantly the knowledge of the *'Cross and the Finished Work of Jesus Christ!'* It is the Word that combats every temptations of the evil one.

2. ***"Then the Devil took Him up into the Holy City and set Him on a pinnacle in the Temple"***

    "And said unto Him, If you are the Son of God (again, the correct translation is since you are the Son of God) cast Yourself down: for it is written, He shall give His Angels charge concerning you: and in their hands they shall bear You up, lest at any time You dash your foot against a stone." Satan tries another tactic in tempting Jesus. He uses a passage of scripture from (Psalm 91:11-12). Once again, this is the place where the believer must know the Word in order to combat this type of temptation.

    Jesus responded saying; ***"It is written again, you shall not tempt the Lord your God."*** Jesus used the passage of scripture from Deut. 6:16. Satan's temptation of Jesus at this juncture was designed to show Jesus Christ not keeping His promises. It was to cast doubt on Him and the Word.

3. ***"Again, the Devil took Him up into an exceeding high mountain and showed Him all the kingdoms of the world and the glory of them."***

    "And said unto Him, All these things will I give You, if You will fall down and worship me." The temptation Satan uses here is for Jesus to by-pass the Cross in which He would gain all things.

Jesus responded saying; *"Get thee hence Satan: for it is written, you shall worship the Lord your God, and Him only shall you serve."*

"Then the Devil left Him, and behold, Angels came and ministered to Him."

Did you notice, every temptation used by the Devil was designed to be appealing to the Lust of the Eye, the Lust of the Flesh, and the Pride of Life? This was certainly not the last of temptations that Christ would face. Life is filled with one temptation after another. However, it is through the Word and one's faith being totally focused on the *'Cross and what Jesus Christ did there!'*

There is the only way, and I mean the only way, for the believer to walk in the 'Newness of Life' which is the abundant life Jesus spoke of in John 10:10. This allows the believer to walk in a victorious life!

'And that way is through the Cross and the Finished Work of Jesus Christ!' (John 19:30; Hebrews 12:2)

CHAPTER 2

The Enemies of Faith Part 2
Ignorance is Deadly

The word **ignorance** is mentioned 18 times in scripture (The Bible) five of those times are in the New Testament (N.T.). The word **ignorant** is mentioned seventeen times fourteen of those times in the N.T. The word **ignorantly** is mentioned four times with two of those times being in the N.T. Within this chapter we are going to reveal just how devastating ignorance can be. There is proof throughout scripture (The Bible) that ignorance can and will keep the believer from living the wellness of life that is intended for them. Before we begin to look into the description and definitions of these three important words let's take a moment and see how Random House Webster's Dictionary defines them.

Ignorance; the state or fact of being ignorant; lack of knowledge or learning.

Ignorant 1. the lack of knowledge or training; unlearned **2.** lacking special; knowledge or information. **3.** uninformed; unaware. **4.** showing lack of knowledge or training.

Ignorantly– doing something through ignorance, illiterate meaning lacking knowledge or in training or it may mean uninformed about a particular subject. An ignorant person can be dangerous. Example, I confess I'm ignorant of higher mathematics." Random House Webster's College Dictionary

As we begin a deeper look into what I consider one of the things that is creating devastation within the lives of believers today, that being **Ignorance.** Let's examine some scriptural references to this subject. Before we do let me say this, we are all ignorant to something, even scriptural and spiritual however, ignorance can be cleared up receiving knowledge within what we have been ignorant of which we will discuss this later in this chapter.

> ***"'My people are destroyed (cut off) for a lack
> of knowledge: because thou hast rejected
> knowledge I will also reject thee, that thou shalt
> be no priest to me: seeing thou hast forgotten the
> law of thy God, I will also forget thy children."
> Hosea 4:6***

There are some important issues that are plaguing the church today:

1. **The lack of knowledge which can be and often is a rejection of knowledge.**

2. **Wrong (incorrect) teaching of the Word.**

3. **Ignorance, which can easily be cleared up through knowledge. However, there seems to be a lack of increasing knowledge that that would within its self**

creates ignorance (lack of understanding) of the Word. This becomes, 'Willful Ignorance.'

In this chapter we are going to deal with both of these problems. In the above passage of scripture there are several statements that need a closer look in order to have a clear understanding.

The phrase *"My people are destroyed"* simply means, they are cut off from the promises that are within the Word of God.

The phrase; *"for a lack of knowledge"* the word *"knowledge"* is from the Hebrew word *"Dhaath"* this noun means knowledge, insight, intelligence understanding. This is being derived from the word the word *"Yada"* meaning to perceive, understand, acquire knowledge. This is a knowledge that engages in the object of that knowledge.

Notice closely the next Phrase; *"because thou hast rejected knowledge"* The word *"rejected"* that would within itself creates ignorance (lack of understanding) of the Word tragedies that fills our world today, and that is a rejection of the truth, which is revealed in the **Cross and what Jesus Christ accomplished there**.

The phrase *"I will reject thee, that thou shalt be no priest to me."* It was the priest that refused a greater knowledge. When the church leaders of today refuse a greater knowledge of the **Cross** and what Jesus Christ accomplished there, the leadership will be stunted in their spiritual growth, while a life of victory will continue to elude them. For Israel it was not only a willful ignorance it was a willful rejection and disregard for the Word of God. They refused to go any deeper in knowledge and personal experience. This is deadly! It totally removed them from the hand of God.

The sadness of Israel being in this position, was the willful ignorance of the priests which trickled down to, and imparted to the people today when we have so many preachers, pastors, teachers delivering a watered down message with sugar and a life that is trouble free, which the scriptures (the Bible), does not teach. The modern day church is rejecting correct biblical knowledge, while, no longer recognizing sin and compromising with a lifestyle that is ungodly. Some are claiming that preaching the cross is preaching death while others are rejecting Jesus Christ as being the **only** path to God. One pastor, who pastors one of, not the largest churches in America, was asked if Jesus Christ was the only way to God and he made the following statement: ***There are many roads that lead to God."*** I find that statement offensive and totally unscriptural, especially, when Jesus said, ***"I am the way the truth and the life: no man cometh unto the Father but by me." (John 14:6)***

<u>Willful Ignorance</u>

What is **willful ignorance**? Willful ignorance is when a person (people) refuses and or rejects knowledge that will remove them from their place and bring about a positive Godly change. It is also willfully rejecting any knowledge of knowledge (the knowledge that I am speaking about here is the Bible and specifically the **"Cross and what Jesus Christ accomplished there)** what is which is a breeding ground for danger.

This kind of ignorance reveals itself when a person falls into a false perception and refuses to go any further, believing they are right, while, believing there is not a need for change, until, no need for change until they have an encounter with the Holy Spirit.

One example is a man named Asaph. Asaph was the leader of worship under the rule of King David. He held a significant spiritual position in Israel (1 Chronicles 16:4-5). He tells of a slippery slope that his own foolishness and ignorance created. His problem began when he became preoccupied with self which led to spiritual distraction. He began to look at the prosperity of the wicked and the suffering of the believers. This trap is as old as Satan himself. Many, if not tens of thousands of Christians have fallen into this same trap.

When reading Psalm 73, Asaph reveals just how distracted he became. His perception of the prosperity of the wicked was extremely clouded. Any time a Christian takes their eyes off of the Word of God and tries to make sense of their own understanding they enter that slippery slope. It was only when Asaph went back to the Sanctuary (the place where God dwelt) and had an encounter with God that his perception (understanding) changed.

> *"Thus my heart was grieved, and I was pricked in my reins." Psalm 73:21*

During his encounter with God, the Holy Spirit began to bring conviction of the sin in which he had fallen. He now comes to the realization of how far he had slipped away. It is only when the Holy Spirit brings conviction to the heart of the believer that they begin to see the sin they have been living in.

"So foolish was I, and ignorant (I did not know):
I was a beast before (with) You." Psalm 73:22

"So foolish, stupid, and brutish was I, and
ignorant: I was like a beast before You." Psalm
73:22 Amplified Bible

The great thing about Asaph was he came to the realization through the Holy Spirit of the error of his ways and repented before God. The sadness that I see in our world today, is, many who have fallen into the trap of willful ignorance refuses to study to remove their ignorance. The scriptures give clear direction to the believer not to fall into this devastating trap.

<u>The Believer of Today is Warned of Not Falling Into This Kind of Ignorance!</u>

"And when He (Jesus Christ) was come near, He
beheld the city and wept over it."

"Saying, If you had known, even you (Israel) at
least in this your day, (This was Jesus speaking
of Himself being the Messiah the Redeemer
which they rejected) the things which "Saying,
If you had known, even you (Israel) at least
in this your day, (This was Jesus speaking
of Himself being the Messiah the Redeemer
which they rejected) the things which belong
unto your peace (Ignorance will keep one from
walking in the promises of God) but now they
are hid from your eyes (Israel allowed a willful
ignorance which brought to them a blindness

concerning the cross and what Jesus Christ was going to accomplish there)." Luke 19: 41-42 Emphasis mine.

As mentioned before, Israel not only displayed a willful ignorance, but, a willful rejection and disregard for the Word of God. The same kind of ignorance is causing defeat in today's believer. Many are now rejecting the **Baptism in the Holy Spirit with the evidence of speaking in tongues.** I have talked to several ministers and pastors who claim to be in the **Pentecostal Faith** yet believe that tongues are no longer for today.

"This I say therefore, and testify in the Lord, that you henceforth walk not as other Gentiles walk in the vanity of their mind (ignorance of spiritual and Divine things of God creates a blindness spiritually and morally)."

"Having the understanding darkened being alienated from the life of God because of the blindness of their heart." Ephesians 4:17-18

Paul is not just speaking of being ignorant concerning the things of God. He was speaking of a willful ignorance, which creates a willful blindness of spiritual things, which in return alienates one from walking in the Divine things of God. This kind of ignorance keeps one from a life of victory.

In 1 Corinthians 10 the apostle Paul warns the believer not to fall into the same ignorance as Israel, who, could not see nor understand how the hand of God was with them and upon them coming out of Egypt. They could not understand how God brought them through and supplied them with their everyday needs. They continued to murmur, grumble and complain until they fell into idolatry. Paul warned the believer to keep their faith in the cross and the finished work of Jesus Christ, for everything that you will ever need was supplied there. The cross is our means and Jesus Christ is our source. The truth is, this is the only arena (within the parameters of the Finished Work of Jesus Christ) that the Holy Spirit works within. A lack of knowledge (ignorance) of the cross and what Jesus Christ did there will keep one from the **Abundant (Newness)** life that Jesus Christ promised (John 10:10; Romans 6:4).

> *"Brethren, my heart's desire and prayer to God for Israel is, that they might be saved."*
>
> *"For I bear them record that they have a zeal of (for) God but not according to knowledge'*
>
> *"Being ignorant (this was willful ignorance) of God's righteousness and going about to establish their own righteousness (living the way they thought was right) having not submitted themselves unto the Righteousness of God*
>
> *"For Christ is the end of the law for Righteousness to everyone who believes" Romans 10:1-4*

Even now Israel fails to recognize Jesus Christ as being the fulfillment of the law (Law of Moses). Through their willful ignorance they are keeping themselves from salvation which is only through the cross and what Jesus Christ accomplished there.

When the cross is no longer the object of one's faith, they will try to live a life established on their own principles and righteousness which is deadly. The sadness here is not only for Israel but for most of the world that falls into willful ignorance of God's plan of salvation and the life that was and is established through Jesus Christ. There are not many roads that lead to salvation, but, **'One and only One,'** which is, **'Jesus Christ and what He for Finished at Calvary!'** Let's take a step deeper.

The word **"ignorance"** is mentioned 18 times in scripture 5 of those times being in the N.T. The word **ignorant** is mentioned 17 times while 14 of those times is used in the N.T. The word **ignorantly** is mentioned 4 times and 2 of those times is in the N.T. There are several Greek words describing ignorance and its derivatives;

1. **Agnoeo** from the neg. a, and neo meaning not to recognize not to know, to be unacquainted with, followed by the prep. **Peri;** concerning; to be ignorant and or having ignorance, concerning something; in the pass. Form; to be unknown, unrecognized, mistaken or misunderstood. (1 Cor. 14:38; 2: 6:9; Gal. 1:22) see also (Acts 17:23; Ro. 1:13; 10:3; 11:25; 1 Cor. 10:1; 12:1; 14:38; 2 Cor. 1:8; 2:11; 1 Thess. 4:13; Heb. 5:2) Also includes the word **ignorantly** which is mentioned two times. (Acts 17:23; 1 Tim. 1:13)

2. **Agonia-** want of knowledge; ignorance which leads to a wrong conduct and forbids the imputation of the guilt to the ignorant individual. (Luke 23:34; Acts 3:17; 17:30; 1 Cor. 2:8; Eph 4:18; 1 Pet. 1:14)

Notice the lack o f true knowledge (ignorance) leads to a life of wrong conduct morally and spiritually. Living a life of this kind of conduct will eventually bring the individual to a place of no guilt for their wrong. According to the apostle Paul this kind of ignorance is the characteristic of heathendom and is a state which renders the need of repentance (Acts 17:30; Eph 4:18)

3. **Agnosa–** not being acquainted with something. Not merely an intellectual, but a moral defect or fault. There is a demonstration of something that is more than an intellectual defect and the supposed knowledge of moral discernment.

   "For so is the will of God, that with well doing
   (to do the good as opposite to missing the mark
   to sin) you may put to silence the ignorance of
   foolish men." 1Peter 2:15; 2:20; 3 John 11.

   This also means to do good so that someone gets a blessing others.

4. **Idiotes–** from *idios* meaning ones own, a common man, as opposite to either a man of power or a man of educational learning. To be uninstructed, unskilled referring to both speech and knowledge. (Acts 4:13 1 Cor. 14:16)

5. **Ianthano–** to be hid, be ignorant of, unaware.

   "For this they willingly are ignorant of, that by
   the Word of God the heavens were of old, and the
   and the earth standing out of the water:"

"Whereby the world that then was, being overflowed with water perished." 2 Peter 3:5-6

Once again, willful ignorance is revealed. However, the apostle Peter admonishes the believer not to fall prey to this kind of ignorance.

"But beloved, be not ignorant of this one thing, that one day is with God as a thousand years, and a thousand years as one day"

The Lord is not slack concerning His Promises, as some men count slackness, but is longsuffering to us-ward not willing that any should perish, but that all should come to Repentance." 2 Peter 3:8-9

Peter expresses that there is no need for ignorance concerning the things of God. God's Divine Promises will be fulfilled. There are times when it may seem that God has forgotten or delayed what He has promised. However, God is preparing you and I along with whosoever will believe and come to repentance for His Divine purpose. See Romans 8:28

<u>The Enemy Preys On Our Ignorance!</u>

"As also in all his (Paul's) epistles speaking in them these things; in which are some things hard to be understood, which they that are unlearned and unstable wrest, as they do also other Scriptures, unto their own destruction." 2 Peter 3:16

The phrase *"As also in all his epistles speaking in them these things"* pertain to the Prophecies and teaching of Paul under the inspiration of the Holy Spirit.

The phrase *"in which are some things hard to be understood"* this possibly refers to Paul's teaching of the Cross and the lack of understanding in-depth of the Finished Work of Jesus Christ. The phrase *"hard to be understood"* means to hardly understand.

The Phrase *"which they that are unlearned and unstable wrest, as they do also the other Scriptures unto their own destruction"* refers to being ignorant and wavering in the faith (Eph. 4: 14; James 1:6-8) it also refers to the twisting and the use of scripture out of its proper context. The phrase *"hard to be understood"* means to hardly understand with the attempt to make the scriptures line up with their own wants and desires. Upon distorting and misrepresenting scripture the ultimate end is destruction.

> *"Ye therefore, beloved, seeing ye know these things before, beware (be cautious and on guard) lest ye also, being led away with the error of the wicked fall from your own steadfastness."*
> *2 Peter 3:17*

The above scripture reveals what the apostle Paul taught was really not that difficult to understand The phrase; *"beware lest ye also, being led away with the error of the wicked"* refers to not leaving the teaching of Jesus Christ and Him crucified along with what He accomplished there, also, to guard oneself concerning other teachings. The last phrase, *"fall from your own steadfastness"* refers to having proper faith in the Cross and what Jesus Christ accomplished there which stabilizes the Believer. (Eph 4; Gal 5:4)

The Challenge!

1. **There are some scriptures that can be difficult to understand.** However, that is the time to go into prayer and allow the Holy Spirit to bring revelation. He can bring that passage alive from a deeper study or from the teaching and or preaching of someone else.

2. **There are some who do not have a desire to learn more therefore, they remain unlearned and unstable.**

3. **There are simply no more excuses for the believing Christian to be ignorant of the Word, especially, concerning the Cross and what Jesus Christ accomplished there.**

4. **As a Born again Believer in Jesus Christ there is no reason not to have an understanding of the Word. Now, this does not mean that you, I, nor anyone else will know all there is to know concerning this great book (the Bible). However, since our body is the Temple of the Holy Spirit and He is the teacher of the Word we should allow the illumination and revelation of the Word to come alive within us!**

CHAPTER 3

The Enemies of Your Faith Part 3 Ignorance of Your Position in Christ

1. **The lack of understanding what it means to be a New Creature in Christ.**

    "Therefore if any man be in Christ, he is a new creature: old things are passed away behold, all things become new." 2 Cor. 5:17

Notice what the scripture does not say; the person in Christ is not the old man reworked; the person in Christ is not placed in a rehabilitation program; the person in Christ is not given over to Humanistic Psychology to solve their inner most problems. But the scripture does say:

A. **The man/woman is a "New Creature in Christ!"** What exactly does that mean? The word **"New"** is from the Greek word **_"Kainos"_** meaning a qualitatively new. It refers to being dedicated and consecrated into a qualitatively new use. There are two other terms that are used in scripture **"be ye transformed"** Ro. 12:2) and **"are changed"** (2 Cor. 3:18) these two terms are from the Greek word ***"Metamorphoo"*** and ***"Metamorphoomai"*** denoting the change of condition and to form. This comes with the idea of a transformation, which, refers to invisible process in Christians which takes place during their life in this age. It is a change within (the inside) and revealed without (on the outside). It also refers to a change that presents one with a qualitatively new use!

B. The word **"creature"** is from the Greek word ***"Ktisis"*** meaning; a founding of a habitable place denoting the individual creature or what has been created. In other words, the believing sinner becomes a **"New Creature"** that Christ can inhabit with the Holy Spirit! ***"Know ye not that ye are the temple of God, and that the Spirit of God dwelleth in you?" (1 Cor. 3:16) "Ye are the temple of the living God"*** (2 Cor. 6:16) Upon being *Born Again* now becomes new in order for God to take up residence!

2. Failure to understand what took place once you were born again.

You Have Been Redeemed.

A. You are Redeemed/Redemption:

There are four Greek words that define **"Redeem/Redemption."**

    a. **Exagoraazo–** this is a verb meaning to buy, to buy out, especially of purchasing a slave with a view to his/her freedom in mind. This also describes the price that is (was) paid to make one free. Thank God that Jesus Christ paid the ultimate price on Calvary for our freedom from sin and gave us eternal life.

b. **Lutroo**– meaning to release on receipt of a ransom. Release by paying a ransom price. In a natural sense of delivering (see Luke 24:21) also setting Israel free from the yoke of the Roman Government.

"But we trusted that it had been He which should have redeemed Israel: and beside all this, today is the third day since these things were done."

In a spiritual sense Titus 2:14, it is becoming free from all iniquity, lawlessness and the bondage of self-will which rejects the will of God.

"Who gave Himself for us, that He might redeem us from all iniquity, and purify unto Himself a peculiar people, zealous of good works."

This is deliverance from the dominion of sin (See Romans 6:14).

Peter reveals that we (the believer) are redeemed from a vain manner of life. 1Peter 1:18

"For as much as ye know that ye were not redeemed with corruptible things, as silver and gold, from your vain conversation received by tradition from your fathers."

Once again, Praise God for redeeming us and for the great price that was paid for our redemption **"The Blood of Jesus Christ.**

c. **Lutrosis** meaning; to bring deliverance through the blood of Jesus Christ (the cross, His death and resurrection) from the guilt and power of sin.

   But with the precious blood of Christ, as of a lamb without blemish and without spot." 1Peter1:18-19

   This is deliverance from the condemnation of sin (See Romans 8:1-2).

   "There is therefore now no condemnation to them which are in Christ Jesus, who walk not after the flesh, but after the Spirit." Romans 8:2

d. **Apolutrosis**– meaning, the deliverance of the believer from the presence and power of sin and of his body from corruption at the coming of the Lord Jesus Christ.

This collectively means as a believer, you have been redeemed from sin and redeemed to God. You are not your own you belong to God. Your body is the temple for the most Holy God (1 Cor. 6:15,19). You are also baptized (placed) in Jesus Christ in His death and resurrection (Romans 6:3-4). You have been redeemed by Jesus Christ through His Finished Work at Calvary!

<u>You Have Been Reconciled</u>

A. You have been Reconciled/ Reconciliation: There is also four Greek words that define Reconcile/ Reconciliation.

   a. Katallasso– properly denotes, to change. Referring to, persons that are changed from enmity to friendship. It is with regard to a relationship between God and man, (2 Corinthians 5:19). In Romans 5:10 it is expressed as not only meaning hostile attitude toward God but it signifies that until this change of attitude takes place men will live under condemnation and be exposed to God's wrath. The finished work of Jesus Christ and the Cross has presented man with the ability to remove this attitude by faith in what Jesus accomplished. This stresses the **Attitude of God** (His Divine Favor) toward us. This is the result of the Atonement! We see this unfolding even to a greater degree in 2 Corinthians 5:18-20.

"And all things are of God, who hath reconciled us to Himself by Jesus Christ, and hath given to us the ministry of reconciliation;

"To wit, that God was in Christ reconciling the world unto Himself, not imputing their trespasses unto them; and hath committed unto us the word of reconciliation."

"Now then we are ambassadors for Christ, as though God did beseech you by us; we pray you in Christ's stead, be ye reconciled to God."

b. **Apokatallasso–** meaning to change from one condition to another, so as to remove all enmity and leave no impediment to unity and peace Ephesians 2:16.

"And that He might reconcile both unto God in one body by the cross, having slain the enmity thereby." Eph. 2:16

In Colossians 1:20-21, notice in verse 20 the word is used of the divine purpose to reconcile through Christ i.e. which is the other part of the Finished Work of Jesus Christ at Calvary (The Cross).

"And, having made peace through the blood of His cross, by Him to reconcile all things unto Himself; by Him I say, whether they be things in earth, or things in heaven".

"And you, that were sometime alienated and enemies in your mind by wicked works, yet now hath He reconciled."

The term **"Having made peace"** speaks of a justifying peace. The term **"Through the Blood of His Cross"** is speaking of the Blood of Jesus Christ satisfying the demands of the law. The term **"by Him to reconcile all things unto Himself"** is speaking of the results of Faith in the Cross. The term **"by Him, I say, whether they be in earth, or things in heaven"** is speaking of the Cross which addresses fallen man and also the Fall of Lucifer.

Source: The Expositor's Study Bible Jimmy Swaggart

c. **Diallasso**– meaning to effect an alteration, to change, to exchange. This is a transformation that changes the quality of a person. It is a qualitative change for a new use. (See Romans 12:2)

"And be not conformed to this world: but be ye transformed by the renewing of your mind, that ye may prove what is that good, and acceptable, and perfect will of God."

d. **Katallage**- meaning; primarily, an exchange, also denotes a reconciliation with change on the part of one party which was induced by the action on the part of another. This reveals Gods, Grace and Love for the person who is in Christ.

"Therefore if any man be in Christ, he is a new creature: old things are passed away; behold, all things are become new." 2 Cor. 5:17

"And, having made peace through the blood of His cross, by Him to reconcile all things unto Himself; by Him I say, whether they be things in earth, or things in heaven".

"And you, that were sometime alienated and enemies in your mind by wicked works, yet now hath He reconciled." Col. 1:20-21

The term **"Having made peace"** speaks of a justifying peace. The term **"Through the Blood of His Cross"** is speaking of the Blood of Jesus Christ satisfying the demands of the law. The term **"by Him to reconcile all**

things unto Himself" is speaking of the results of Faith in the Cross. The term **"by Him, I say, whether they be in earth, or things in heaven"** is speaking of the Cross which addresses fallen man and also the Fall of Lucifer.

Source: The Expositor's Study Bible Jimmy Swaggart

Because of what Jesus Christ did at Calvary today's believer is seated together with Him in Heavenly Places. Notice, Ephesians 1:18-23

The phrase; *"The eyes of your understanding being enlightened (Refers to the Holy Spirit bringing to light understanding within the believers heart)."*

The phrase; *"That you may know what is the hope of His calling (there is a genuine hope and it is within what Jesus Christ did at Calvary.)"*

The Phrase; *"and what is the riches of the glory of His inheritance in the Saints (the Saints are Gods inheritance which reveals the riches of His glory)" Verse 18*

The phrase; *"And what is the exceeding greatness of His power to us-ward who believe (refers to the ability to in the Newness of Life through the power of the Holy Spirit)."*

The phrase; *"According to the working of His mighty power (this is referring exclusively of the Cross and the Finished Work of Jesus Christ)." Verse 19*

The phrase; *"Which He wrought in Christ, when He raised Him from the dead (refers to God the Father Who resurrected Jesus Christ through the power of the Holy Spirit)."*

The phrase; *"and set Him at His Own Right Hand in the Heavenly places (refers to God the Father receiving the Sacrifice of Jesus Christ and positioned Him in the highest place of honor and authority)." Verse 20*

"Far above all principality, and powers, and might, and dominion, and every name that is named in this world, but also in that which is to come." Verse 21 this verse reveals the name and exaltation of Jesus Christ which was accomplished at the Cross of Calvary!

The phrase; *"And has put all things under His feet (this is the fulfillment of Gen. 3:15 and brings to life the original purpose of the creation of man)."*

The phrase; *"and gave Him to be the Head over all things to the Church (Jesus Christ was given supreme authority headship over all things. He is the Head of the Church because of what He Finished at Calvary)." Verse 22*

The phrase; *"Which is His body (the Church is the Body of Jesus Christ and He is the source of life within the Church)." and fills it with His presence through the person of the Holy Spirit*

Let's take this a step further, which is revealed in Ephesians 2:5:6

> *"Even when we were dead in sins, hath quickened us together with Christ, (by grace you are saved)"*

The phrase; ***"Even when we were dead in sins"*** is from the Greek word, ***"Praptoma"*** meaning; purposely stepping over. This is simply missing of that which is right, involving little action. It is the revealing of the sinner being in a place where they could not help themselves.

The phrase; ***"hath quickened us together with Christ"*** is referring to the ***'Newness of life' (Romans 6:4)*** which is imparted to the believer through the resurrection of Jesus Christ. The identity of the believer is now in Christ and the **'Abundant life'** Jesus spoke of in John 10:10.

The Apostle Paul states; ***"For if we have been planted together in the likeness of His death we shall be also in the likeness of His resurrection." Romans 6:5***

The believer can now live and walk in a ***'Resurrected Life,'*** only with the understanding of the ***'likeness of His death,'*** which, is to understand what Jesus Christ accomplished at Calvary. This of course, is an understanding that Satan and his minions fight so desperately against. He certainly does not want you and I to come to the knowledge of the ***'Finished Work of Jesus Christ at the Cross!'*** Coming into and receiving knowledge of the Cross and what Jesus Christ Finished there, opens up a new world of the ***'Newness of Life!'***

'Grace' of God that man can come to salvation. Notice, it is a positive statement, there is no ***'Shall be, Hope to be* or *Will be saved,'*** it is a statement of assurance, ***'You Are Saved!'***

The phrase; ***"And hath (has) raised us up together"*** is speaking of coming alive spiritually in Christ. This also speaks of what

Jesus Christ accomplished at Calvary and the benefits of the believer. The phrase; *'Raised us up,'* is speaking of the great gift of *'Salvation,'* and all of its benefits, such as; Justification and Sanctification. The believing sinner is *'Raised up'* to a life of victory!

The phrase; *"And made us sit together,"* first the phrase, *'made us'* is referring to a positive act that takes place when one is in Christ Jesus. The phrase, *'sit together'* is connected to the Greek word, *'sunkathizo'* which has been translated *"seated us with Him!"* the word *'sit'* indicates a work that has been finished. The word, *'together'* is speaking of being in Christ and Him in you and being in the position He is in which is at the right hand of the Father.

The phrase; *'in heavenly places'* not only does this speak of where Christ is now, it also reveals that the thinking of the believer should be one of **'Victory' i.e. *'Throne Victory'*** which is the spiritual position of the believer. This is the reason why the Holy Spirit is continually working on the believers *'Condition to meet their Spiritual Position!'*

Satan's Avenue of Attack Against Man!

"The thief comes not, but to steal, and to kill, and to destroy" John 10:10a

The thief (Satan) uses any method he can to derail you and I from the object of our faith, that being in the *'Cross and the Finished* Work of Jesus Christ!'*

Satan tries to bring different ways to get to God, while, there is only one way and that through Jesus Christ and Him only. He will also use the weaknesses of the flesh to war and tempt the believer (James 1:14-15). One of his greatest tools is using deceit to derail the believer (Eph. 4:14). Another thing that he likes to do is cause confusion of the Word which results in unbelief (Mark 9:14-24). He will use the sin nature of man to beset (derail) him from his walk in the faith (Heb. 12:1). Lastly, he will do whatever he can to get the believer to waver in his faith (Eph. 4:14; James 1:6). The sad fact is, his methods seem to be working, not only in the world but also in the Modern day Church. Many are being derailed by the methods that the evil one has placed before them without realizing the error of their way!

Get knowledge of the Word and derail all of Satan's attacks and live a life of Victory!

CHAPTER 4

The Enemies of Faith Part 4
The Battle to Overcome Ignorance

There is an upside of being ignorant. Think about it, we are all ignorant to some things, that is, unless we know everything, which is totally impossible. I have used this statement many times over the years *"I would rather be ignorant than stupid because ignorance can be taught but stupid thinks it knows everything about something!"* There is the upside to ignorance, it can be cleared up and removed through knowledge. However, in this case I am not speaking of a natural knowledge but spiritual knowledge. Notice the following;

> **"But as it is written, eye hath not seen, nor ear heard, neither have entered into the heart of man, the things which God hath prepared for them that love Him." 1 Corinthians 2:9**

I have heard this scripture literally butchered over the years without paying close attention to what the apostle Paul said. Paul is quoting a passage from Isaiah 64:4 which, is dealing the nation of Israel not be able to see, hear, the great promises that God has prepared for the believers with the New Covenant. The purpose behind this great passage of scripture, is, to reveal to man the impossibility to see, comprehend, and come to an understanding of the greatness of God.

> *"For what man knoweth the things of man, save the spirit of man which is in him? Even so the things of God knoweth no man, but the Spirit of God. 1 Corinthians 2:11*

The apostle Paul makes it extremely clear in this scripture that with the knowledge that man may possess he still cannot know God nor understand anything about Him. Man may know and understand another man because he is of the spirit of man. However, man can never know God nor come to any understanding of what God has prepared for the believer within his own reasoning. Yet, there is a way for the believer to begin to see, hear, and perceive the things of God. Notice the last statement in verse 11;

"Even so the things of God knoweth no man, but by the Spirit God." The only way that man can even begin to see and or know God is through and by the Holy Spirit. This brings us to verse 10.

"But God hath revealed them unto us by His Spirit: for the Spirit searcheth all things, of God." The phrase *"But God hath revealed them"* is from the Greek word *Apokalupto* meaning to literally remove a veil or covering exposing to open view what was before hidden; to make manifest or reveal a thing previously secret or unknown (Luke 2:35; 1 Corinthians 3:13).

For an example, the O.T. is the N.T. concealed and the N.T. is the O.T. revealed (2 Corinthians11-18).

God has now removed the veil to open up and reveal those things which man's eye's have not seen, his ear's not heard, nor his mind able to comprehend, nor his heart able to receive. The phrase *"unto us by His Spirit"* reveals the way in which God imparts His Word and makes it alive. It is the Holy Spirit that brings knowledge and imparts (reveals and illuminates) the spiritual things of God. There is no other way to receive any knowledge of the things of God.

The phrase *"for the Spirit seareth all things, yea, the deep things of God."* The Holy Spirit is the one (the very vehicle) who brings to light the Word of God. Who better to reveal God and the things of God for He (The Holy Spirit) is God.

I have often said that I am glad that the Holy Spirit got me before men could poison me with their doctrine. Many years ago when I began in the ministry I would lay on my face for untold hours, everyday, seeking God and the things of God. The Holy Spirit began to unveil and illuminate the Word to me. Of course God has used anointed men and women in my life to teach and guide into the truth of the Word. There are great preachers and teachers of the Word today that are bringing forth revelation of the Word under the direction of the Holy Spirit. However, there are also those that are spreading poison and the believer today must know the difference and that only comes through and by the Holy Spirit.

Clearing up ignorance was extremely important to the apostle Paul as we have made mentioned previously. Matter of fact He used this term eleven times. Previously we mentioned Paul using it to avoid a willing ignorance, now, let's look at how Paul admonishes the believer to go into a deeper depth concerning the things of God.

1. **He wanted the believers in Rome to understand how important it was for him to come and help them grow in the Word concerning the Cross and the Grace of God. (Romans 1:13)**

2. **He did not want the Gentiles to fall into the same spiritual state as Israel. (Romans 10:3; 11:25)**

3. **He did not want the believer to be ignorant concerning the Truths of the Word. (1 Cor. 10:1-11)**

4. **He did not want the believers to be ignorant concerning the gifts of the Holy Spirit. (1 Cor. 12:1)**

5. **He had concerns about men remaining ignorant and it costing them their soul. (1 Cor. 14:38)**

6. **He wanted the believers to understand the trouble which he encountered in Asia, however the scripture does not go into detail. (2 Cor. 1:8)**

7. **He did not want the believer to be ignorant of the devices of Satan. (2 Cor. 2:11)**

8. **He did not want the believer to be ignorant concerning the rapture of the church. (1 Thess. 4:13)**

9. **He revealed how in his unbelief he acted ignorantly and received mercy. (1Tim. 1:13)**

10. **He speaks of having compassion for those who are ignorant.**

The apostle Peter was also concerned about the believer remaining in ignorance.

1. **Don't allow one to be ruled by the sin nature through ignorance. (1 Pet. 1:14)**

2. **Put a stop to foolishness. (1Pet. 2:15)**

3. **Peter speaks of a willful ignorance concerning the creation. (2 Pet. 3:5-7)**

4. **Peter expresses to the believer to not be ignorant to spiritual things and the way God operates. (2Pet. 3:8)**

Luke spoke of ignorance getting in the way of spiritual progress. (Acts 3:17; 4:13)

1. **In speaking of the crucifixion of Jesus Christ to the Men of Israel:**

   "And now, brethren, I reckon that through ignorance you did it, as did also your rulers."
   Acts 3:17

2. Peter was speaking of a **willful ignorance.** They did not have any desire to learn about Jesus Christ. **In speaking of the boldness and the anointing of Peter and John:**

"Now, when they saw the boldness of Peter and John and perceived that they were unlearned and ignorant men, they marveled and they took knowledge of them, that they had been with Jesus." Acts 4:13

Their perception of Peter and John being unlearned and ignorant was due to knowing that they had not attended any formal training in the Schools of the Rabbi's. Their perception was so off course because Peter and John were far from being unlearned and ignorant. Because of the boldness and the anointing upon these great men they came to the realization that they had been with Jesus Christ. This brings us to some things to consider on how to remove the ignorance that we may have concerning the things and ways of God.

The Challenge!

1. **We cannot lean on our own understanding.**

2. **We must give the Holy Spirit the latitude to teach and reveal the Word. (Luke 12:12; 1 Cor. 2:10; (Proverbs 3:5) The revelation of the Word must come from the Holy Spirit.**

3. **Study, study, study. (2 Timothy 2:15) However, upon studying the Word you cannot twist the scriptures to fit in with your opinions/ideas. You must allow the Word to say what it says without any compromise.**

4. **There must be a hunger for God and His ways. (Exodus 33:11-23; Psalm 42:1)**

5. **The object of your faith must be in the Cross and the Finished Work of Jesus Christ! (Luke 9:23; John 8:31-36)**

6. **There must be an understanding of the cross and what Jesus Christ accomplished there. We will discuss this in a great degree in a following chapter. (1 Cor. 1:17-18; 23)**

There Are Just No More Excuses!

It is vital that every believer strive for an understanding of God, His Word, His character, His being. There also must be an understanding of what Jesus Christ accomplished at Calvary along with the mechanics and the dynamics of the Holy Spirit. Please understand what I am saying. When I talk about clearing and removing ignorance concerning the things of God, it is just the starting point. When we (the believer) allow the Holy Spirit to teach us it is like being in a lifelong experience of being in His class room. There is nobody that will ever know it all but the learning process is (should be) exciting!

The greatest tragedy of all is being ignorant concerning Jesus Christ and what He accomplished at Calvary. It goes deeper than just the saving of one's soul. **His Work is Finished** it is now time that you pick up your Cross and follow Him! (Luke 9:23)

CHAPTER 5

Fight The Good Fight!

"Fight the good fight of faith, lay hold on eternal life, whereunto thou art called, and has professed a good profession before many witnesses" 1 Timothy 6:12

The Apostle Paul was giving the young evangelist Timothy valuable information concerning his faith walk. It is important to notice, the fight the Apostle was referring to was one of faith. The fight that is going on around every believer is one of faith. The enemy will try anything and everything possible to distract, discourage, derail and remove you (the believer) from the correct walk of faith. He will try to remove you (the believer) from the correct object of faith. Which is the Cross and the Finished Work of Jesus Christ!

Within the above passage of scripture, the Apostle Paul gives some instruction on how to fight this great fight of faith.

The phrase, *"Fight the good fight"* the word *"Fight"* is from the Greek word *"Agonizomai"* *"Ag-o-nid'-zom-ahee"* with the idea to struggle, lit, (fight for the prize) fig. (to contend with an adversary) or gen. (to endure in order to accomplish something): to fight, labor, fervently, to strive, to contend for victory. The task of faith is to persevere amid temptation and opposition.

The Apostle Paul was very familiar with the Greek games along with the athletes. He often used the games to bring an illustration of the spiritual battle that every Christian will face (1 Cor. 9:24-27). The Romans lived and thrived upon these games.

When there was a boxing match, the boxers would often use boxing gloves that consisted of fur lining the inside to make it comfortable. The outside of the gloves was made of ox-hide mingled with lead and iron. The idea was to mar the face and put out the eyes of the opponent.

This fight was serious indeed. It is a great analogy of the spiritual fight that the believer is engaged in. It is so serious that the enemy of your (our) faith desires to kill, steal and destroy. It is a fight to the death!'

The phrase *"the good fight"* is from the Greek word *"Kalos"* *"kal-os"* comes with the idea of, beautiful, but chiefly (fig.) good (lit. or morally) i.e. valuable and or virtuous. To be honest, balanced and complete. In other words, this is a fight that must be fought legally. The believer has received the legal right to fight this great fight because of the Cross and what Jesus Christ accomplished there. Matter of fact, this will be the only direction that the Holy Spirit leads you into this fight. Everything He (the Holy Spirit) does is with the parameters of the Cross! (Romans 8)

The Apostle Paul said it this way;

> *"The desperate, straining, agonizing contests, marked by its beauty of technique, I, like a wrestler, have fought to a finish, and at present am resting in its victory" (2 Tim. 4:7)*

The word, *"fight"* in this scripture comes with an interesting twist which explain in greater detail why the Apostle Paul used the games and the athletes that were involved. The word comes from the Greek word, *"Agon" "ag-one"* meaning a place of assembly (by impl.) a contest (held there), fig, an effort or anxiety: a conflict, contention, fight or race; implying a force or violence, strife, contention for victory or mastery, such as pertaining to the Greek games of running, boxing, or wrestling.

This fight certainly is not a pretty one and can get very messy at times. However, if the believer can get a revelation and understanding of the Cross of Calvary and the Victory that Jesus Christ won there, they (we) would understand that we are fighting against a foe that has already been defeated!

The phrase *"lay hold on eternal life"* the words *"lay hold"* is from the Greek word *"epilambanomia"* meaning to seize (for any purpose, lit. or fig. to catch, lay hold (on) (up) to take by holding on to and refusing to let go. This is the idea of taking hold of and refusing to let go of the **"Finished Work of Jesus Christ at Calvary!"**

> *"And He (Jesus Christ) said to them all, (all who would here the Message of the Cross), if any man will come after me(pertaining to all who will come to Him for salvation), let him deny himself (to remove himself from working and living in one's own ability, understanding, and strength), take up his cross (start living in the victor and abundant life that Christ won at Calvary (John 10:10; Romans 6:1-4), daily (everyday take up what the Cross accomplished), and follow me (Jesus Christ is the only way to salvation and a life of victory!) (John 8:31-36; 10:10; 14:6)*

> *"Beloved, when I gave all diligence to write unto you of the common salvation, it was needful for me to write unto you, and exhort you that ye should earnestly contend for the faith which was once delivered unto the saints." Jude 3*

There had been many false teachers who had entered the Church. Their false doctrine led many into a state of apostasy leading them away from the Cross of Christ as being the only way to salvation. This is much like the Modern day Church which is currently present. The two major questions that needed answered were; **"What are we fighting for?"** and **"What or who are we fighting against?"**

We are fighting against the forces of sin that would remove us from the salvation that Jesus Christ bought for us!

We are fighting to stand in **"The Faith"** of the Cross and what Jesus Christ accomplished there to remain as the **"Focus of our Faith!"**

The word *"contend"* is from the Greek word *"Epagonizomia"* meaning to strive; contend earnestly; to fight for in reference to something with the idea of that which gives the occasion.

When I think of someone contending for something my mind takes me to a man by the name of Shammah. This great man, who was one of David's mighty men, continued to stand in the middle of his lentil patch and fight the enemy. He refused to give up and give away what was his! He won a great victory! (see 2 Sam. 23:11-12

Just as Shammah stood his ground and fought the good fight, so must you fight to stay within the victory that Jesus Christ has won and given to all who will believe. (See John 3:16).

I am in no way saying that this fight is easy. However, I am saying that through the Cross and the Finished Work of Jesus Christ every believer has received the strength, ability and the proper tools to continue in **The Faith!**

Stand your ground! In the following pages we are going to deal with how to stand against the enemy of your (our) faith and come out on the winning side!

<u>Teach Me To Fight</u>

> *"Blessed be the Lord my strength, which teacheth my hands to war, and my fingers to fight."*
> *Psalm 144:1*

King David penned this Psalm after the rising of rebellion from Absalom.

"When men become eminent for things to which they were not regularly educated and for which they have had but very few advantages, they should be more deeply sensible that God has been their **Teacher.** Though courage, military skill and success are gifts of the Creator, they are seldom so employed as to warrant the use of these words, '**He Teacheth**'. Too generally the great murderer instigates ambitious men to destroy their fellow creatures without a cause. Happy are those whom the Lord teacheth to fight the good fight of faith and gives that noblest victory conquest of dominion over their spirits."

Matthew Henry Commentary with the comments of Thomas Scott, page 327

It is important to understand who the teacher is in order to fight the proper fight the proper way. In Psalm 144 it is clear Who (God) taught David the **"Good Fight of Faith"** that brought him many great victories. Every believer needs this teaching because the fight we are in is not against flesh and blood but against principalities, powers, and rulers of darkness of this world, against spiritual wickedness in high places (Eph. 6:12) which we will discuss in the following chapter. Our fight is the fight to Stay in the Faith!

The following are some training tips on just how to fight the good fight.

1. **Identify the Conflict:**

    A. **Where is the conflict coming from? (Eph.6)**

    B. **Examine each level of the conflict. (Eph.6)**

C. What or who is behind the conflict? 2 Cor. 11:24-30; 12:1-8

D. What weapons are being used against you and how must you stand and fight? (2Cor.12:9)

2. Have a plan of attack, see;

A. Joshua 1:8

B. Jehoshaphat 2 Chr.20

C. David facing Goliath 1 Sam. 17:22-50

3. Fight the good (Legal) fight.

A. You will need spiritual discernment to understand what the attack is, where it is coming from and what weapons are needed to fight and stay.

B. Allow the Holy Spirit to reveal what is involved in the attack.

4. Take possession of the benefits of the "Finished Work of Jesus Christ at Calvary!

A. Caleb after 45 years still said give me this mountain! He held onto the promises of God and never let go of his faith. (Joshua 14:6-12

"It is God that girdeth me with strength, and maketh my way perfect."

"He maketh my feet like hinds feet, and setteth
me upon my high places."
"He teacheth my hands to war, so that a bow of
steel is broken by mine arms."
See Also Psalm 144:1

JUST A REMINDER!

When the Cross and what Jesus Christ accomplished there is the focus of one's faith, they are sure to walk in victory! The apostle Paul penned the way he kept the faith!

"I have fought a good fight (should have been translated, "I have fought the good fight." Paul fought his fight with sin to a finish, and was resting in a complete victory), I have finished my course (I have been faithful in carrying out that which had been assigned to him), I have kept the faith (refers to the deposit of Truth regarding the meaning ofthe Cross and the Resurrection of Christ, with which the Lord had entrusted Paul):"
The Expositor's Study Bible Jimmy Swaggart,

The word, *'Fought'* is from the Greek word, *'Agonizomia'* meaning; to contend for victory, especially in the public games (1 Cor. 9:25). It also refers to the task of faith in persevering amid temptations and opposition. To take pains, to wrestle as in a prize contest making every effort to achieve the goal. It also refers to, standing against the hindrances that come in the development of the Christian life. **THIS IS A FIGHT THAT IS FOUGHT TO WIN AND NOT A FIGHT TO KEEP FROM LOOSING!**

The word, *'Fight'* is from the Greek word, **'Agon'** the verb, *'ago'* implies fighting with force or violence, to strife or contention, to contend viguorsly. It is a contest or mastery such as seen in the Greek games, i.e. running, boxing or wrestling. It applies to the struggles with the life of the believer.

The word, *'Good'* is from the Greek word, *'Kaios'* meaning; constitutionally good without being benevolent; it expresses a harmonious, complete, fight with a balanced proportion. (John 2:10; James 2:7) **IT IS A LEGAL FIGHT WITH THE BACKING OF THE WORD OF GOD!**

THIS IS THE KIND OF FAITH FIGHT THAT GAVE THE APOSTLE PAUL THE ABILITY TO KEEP THE FAITH! NOTICE THE FOLLOWING CONCERNING PAUL'S FAITH FIGHT;

> **I was beaten of the Jews Five times with Thirty-nine stripes. I KEPT THE FAITH!**
>
> **Three times I was beaten with rods, yet, I KEPT THE FAITH!**
>
> **Once when Silas and I were in Philippi and were thrown in jail, at the midnight hour we began to sing praises to God(Acts 16-25) We KEPT THE FAITH!**
>
> **When I was in Lystra the Jews from Antioch and Iconium persuaded the people to stone me. I was thrown out of the city and left for dead. YET, I CONTINUED TO KEEP THE FAITH!**

Three times I suffered shipwreck, once on my way to Italy (Acts 27). I STILL KEPT THE FAITH!

I spent a night and a day in the sea, YET, I NEVER LOST THE FAITH! I CONTINUED TO KEEP THE FAITH:

In my travels!
In perils of water!
In perils of Robbers!
In Perils by mine own countrymen!
In Perils by the heathen!
In perils in the city!
In perils in the wilderness!
In perils in the sea!
In perils among false brethren!

I CONTINUED TO KEEP THE FAITH!!!

CONCLUSION

<u>**How to fight the good fight and keep the faith!**</u>

1. When I do not know what to do, I STAND STILL IN HIS STRENGTH AND AUTHORITY AND IN THE POWER OF HIS MIGHT!

2. When I feel myself begin to waver, I GIRD MY LOINS WITH THE BELT OF TRUTH THAT MAKES ME STABLE!

3. When I feel my heart is not right, I PUT ON THE BREASTPLATE OF RIGHTEOUSNESS! It makes my heart right to forgive!

4. When I feel my feet begin to slip, I SHOD MY FEET WITH THE PREPARATION OF THE GOSPEL OF PEACE! They will continue to guide my path!

5. When accusations come my way and the enemy begins to fire his darts of temptation, I RAISE THE SHIELD OF FAITH! It will quench (PUT A STOP TO) all the fire from the enemy!

6. When negative thoughts and vain imaginations begin to arise, I PUT ON THE HELMET OF SALVATION! It clears and renews my mind and protects me from all evil thinking!

7. When the enemy stands and yells and screams Stop, I DRAW THE SWORD OF THE SPIRIT WHICH IS THE WORD OF GOD AND IS MY DEFENSE!

8. I FIGHT THE GOOD FIGHT OF FAITH BY PRAYING WITHOUT CEASING!!! Eph. 6:10-18

Continue to fight your battles with praise and worship with hands raised allowing God to fight for you!

Moses; the battle against Amalek; Exodus 17:8-16

Jehoshaphat; the battle against, the Moabites, the Ammonites and Mt Seir. 2 Chr. 20

Paul ad Silas imprisoned at Philippi; Act 16: 16-31

THIS IS THE WAY TO FIGHT YOUR BATTLES!

ABOUT THE AUTHOR

Dr. Baldock is the founder/president of *"Gaining The Victory Ministries."* He is currently in his fiftieth year of ministry.

Dr. Baldock began his ministry in March of 1971. In March of 1973, he began in full time ministry. He and his wife Julie have been married for thirty-six years. Together they have seven grown children, Rick, Tammy, Tracy, Rhonda, Alicia, Michael and Ashley. He and Julie also have several grandchildren and great-grandchildren.

Dr. Baldock has pastored nine churches; four of which he pioneered and built from the ground floor up. Dr. Baldock also has four earned Doctorate Degrees, and one Honorary Doctorate.

He is currently traveling around to different churches teaching and preaching the word of God. He is currently attending The Sanctuary Church in Beech Grove/Indianapolis, Indiana. Dr. Baldock has spoke at many conventions and has worked with several well known ministries. He taught for several years with the International College of Bible Theology and with Midwest Seminary. He has taught undergraduate and graduate school. He taught at the School of the Prophets in Poplar Bluff,

Missouri for about four years, and he taught about two to three years at The Lion of Judah in Malden, Missouri.

Dr. Baldock also traveled to Malawi in East Africa and, for thirteen days he, and two other ministers trained over one hundred and twenty-five church leaders.

Dr. Baldock is a gifted preacher and teacher of the Word of God. His heartbeat is in helping to restore those who have fallen on hard times and are in need of mentoring. He also enjoys teaching and training leaders within the local church.

Dr. Baldock has authored many books and study helps. He believes that the gifts that God has given him should be shared and imparted to others. He believes that everyday practical teaching will reveal the application of the Word of God in the person's everyday living. He is a strong believer in the fact that everything you will ever receive from God is because of the **"Cross"** and **"The finished work of Jesus Christ."** He believes that the **"Cross"** is the means of all you will ever need, and **"Jesus Christ is the Source"** of all God has supplied for those that believe!

Dr. Baldock is available to speak and teach at your local church or, conferences, along with leadership training and motivational speaking. If you would like for Dr. Baldock to come and speak at your church or conference, and if you would like more information about his books, CD's, DVD's and a plethora of teaching tools, you can write to:

Gaining the Victory Ministries Inc.

Dr. Mike Baldock
P.O. Box 648
Spencer, Indian 47460

Or, you can e-mail him at:
gainingvictoryministries@gmail.co.

Or visit our web site at;
Gtvministries.com